Light
and
Its
Effects

Jenna Winterberg

Consultant

Michael Patterson
Principal Systems Engineer

Publishing Credits

Rachelle Cracchiolo, M.S.Ed., *Publisher*
Conni Medina, M.A.Ed., *Managing Editor*
Diana Kenney, M.A.Ed., NBCT, *Senior Editor*
Dona Herweck Rice, *Series Developer*
Robin Erickson, *Multimedia Designer*
Timothy Bradley, *Illustrator*

Image Credits: Cover, p.1 Shutterstock; p.19 Birgit
Tyrrell / Alamy; pp.19, 22 Courtney Patterson; pp.6, 17, 18
GIPhotoStock / Science Source; p.25 GL Archive / Alamy;
p.16 imageBROKER / Alamy; pp.3, 4, 5, 7, 8, 9,11, 12, 14,
18, 19, 20, 27, 30, 32 iStock; pp.28, 29 Janelle Bell-Martin;
p.19 Leon Swart / Alamy; p.20 Photoshot Holdings Ltd
/ Alamy; p.23 Science Photo Library / Alamy; all other
images from Shutterstock.

Library of Congress Cataloging-in-Publication Data

Winterberg, Jenna, author.
  Light and its effects / Jenna Winterberg.
    pages cm
  Summary: "Light can travel faster than anything else
in the universe. It makes it possible for you to wear a
different colored shirt every day. But what exactly is
light and where does it come from? One thing is for sure,
light makes our world a brighter place."-- Provided by
publisher.
  Audience: Grades 4 to 6.
  Includes index.
  ISBN 978-1-4807-4685-5 (pbk.)
  1. Light--Juvenile literature. 2. Wave theory of light--
Juvenile literature. I. Title.
  QC360.W56 2016
  535--dc23
                          2014045208

Teacher Created Materials

5301 Oceanus Drive
Huntington Beach, CA 92649-1030
http://www.tcmpub.com
ISBN 978-1-4807-4685-5
© 2016 Teacher Created Materials, Inc.
Printed in China
Nordica.082019.CA21901024

Table of Contents

Light in the Universe

We wake up when light streams through our windows in the morning. We know our day will wind down after sunset. We turn on the lights first thing in the morning, turning them off only when our day is done. So, of course, we know what light is.

At least, we assume we know what light is. But ask yourself, "What makes up light?"

Most things in the universe are made up of **matter**. Matter is made up of tiny particles called *atoms*. Light can behave just like one of these particles. But light isn't matter, and it doesn't always work like a particle, either. Instead, it acts like a wave.

Light is a special form of energy. It can move faster than anything else in the universe. It can travel in a straight path, or it can bend and turn. And it can even pass through objects.

Even though we think we understand light because it's all around us, there's a lot more to it than meets the eye.

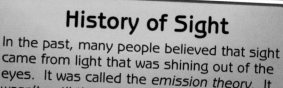

History of Sight

In the past, many people believed that sight came from light that was shining out of the eyes. It was called the *emission theory*. It wasn't until the eleventh century that this theory changed. When a scientist named Ibn al-Haytham published his findings, people finally started to understand the truth about sight. He said that light reflects off objects and goes into the eyes to create sight.

Waves of Light

We often think of water when we see the word *waves*. But light can travel in waves, too. In the same way a ribbon ripples when it's tugged from one end, waves have an up-and-down pattern. Even though we can see light, we can't see these waves.

Sunlight takes time to travel to Earth. The light we see is actually from 8 minutes and 20 seconds ago!

Light

We don't think of light as having much of an appearance. That's because **white light**, like the light the sun gives off, seems colorless. In truth, white light contains a spectrum, or range, of colors. If you were to break it up to see all of its parts, you would find a rainbow of color. It contains red, orange, yellow, green, blue, indigo, and violet!

When we observe light, we're really observing electromagnetic radiation. Light has wavelengths that we can see. A wavelength is the measure of distance between two peaks of the same wave. Of all the colors that make up the **visible spectrum**, red has the longest wavelength. Violet has the shortest. But visible light is just a small part of a range we call the *electromagnetic spectrum*. We can't see the other wavelengths in this range, but we can observe them.

Indoor Rainbow

To split light into a visible spectrum, fill a container with water. Then, move it into a sunlit window. Place a small mirror in the water, and angle it toward the sun. A rainbow will appear on the wall!

The Rest of the Spectrum

Ultraviolet (UV) waves have shorter wavelengths and more energy than visible light. Our skin absorbs UV rays, sometimes causing a sunburn. We can't see these rays, but they can damage our skin and our eyes.

X-rays have shorter wavelengths and even more energy. They don't just seep into skin. They pass through it! So, we use them to look at our bones. They are also used to inspect luggage at airports.

The wave with the shortest wavelength is the **gamma ray**. It has the most energy of any wave. It's so powerful it can kill cells. We often use it to eliminate cancer cells from the body.

On the other end of the spectrum is **infrared**. Infrared has a longer wavelength and less energy than visible light. We can detect its energy when we feel heat from fire. We use this wave in remote controls. We also use it in night-vision goggles. We even use it to toast bread!

The wavelengths of microwaves are even longer. These waves help us send information through space with satellites. They even help us cook! In fact, the microwave appliance uses this wave and was named after it.

Radio waves have the longest wavelength and the least energy. We communicate with them because their length allows them to reach places other waves can't. They can even bend around obstacles, such as houses.

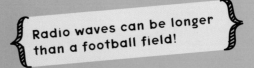
Radio waves can be longer than a football field!

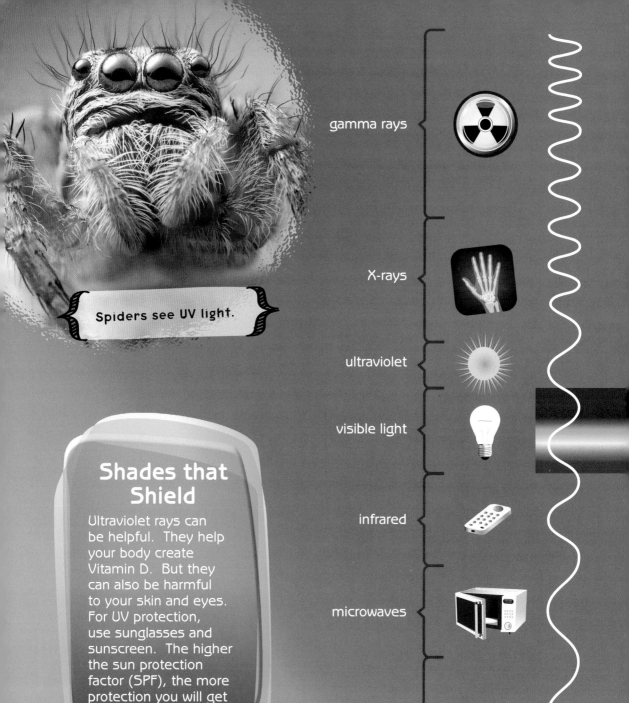

Spiders see UV light.

gamma rays

X-rays

ultraviolet

visible light

infrared

microwaves

radio waves

Shades that Shield

Ultraviolet rays can be helpful. They help your body create Vitamin D. But they can also be harmful to your skin and eyes. For UV protection, use sunglasses and sunscreen. The higher the sun protection factor (SPF), the more protection you will get from harmful rays.

Traveling Light

Light waves don't just float around us randomly. They all come from a source. The sun is a light source. A flashlight is another. You don't usually use your television or computer to light up a room, but they're light sources, too.

Reflection

Not every object is a light source. But all objects reflect light. That reflected light enables us to see the object while also giving it color.

When white light bounces off a red marble, not all the light is reflected—only the red waves. The marble absorbs the remaining colors of the visible spectrum.

Every surface absorbs and reflects different wavelengths, giving each object its unique color. White surfaces reflect all colors. That's why they appear so bright. Objects with black surfaces absorb almost all colors.

Feel the Heat

When sun's energy is absorbed, it creates heat. That's why your skin gets warm in the sun.

Seeing Things

Why can we see things when it's light out but not when it's dark? Light hits objects and bounces off them. When the light reaches our eyes, we can see the object. Without light, we can't see!

All light travels in a straight line. Radio waves are able to curve around objects due to their extremely long wavelengths. Visible light has no such advantage. When it strikes something that is **opaque**, or solid, the object blocks the light's path. It absorbs or reflects the light. A shadow forms where the light would have continued on its path. That's why shadows always appear on the opposite side of a light source.

But not all objects are opaque. Glass, for example, allows light to pass through. That's why we have windows in our homes. See-through objects, such as glass, are often **transparent**. They don't cast shadows. They simply allow light to continue along its path. In other words, they transmit light.

Stained glass windows have colored glass that is translucent.

When an object is only partly transparent, we call it **translucent**. One example is a colored balloon. The balloon blocks some of the light. Thus, it casts a shadow. It also lets some light through. So, the shadow contains color reflected from the balloon.

translucent

opaque

transparent

Making stained glass is an ancient art that can be traced back to the early Egyptians.

Refraction

Visible light casts shadows because it can't curve around solid objects. It must follow a straight path. But there are two instances when visible light can bend or change direction. Reflection is the first instance. The second is called *refraction*.

Refraction occurs when light moves from one material to another, such as from air to water. In this case, water slows the light. That makes objects in water appear different than normal. For example, a fish may look larger than it really is. Or an object only partly in water might look broken where the water meets the air. These odd visual effects are the result of light waves bending.

Rainbows are also produced by refraction. The sun hits water in the air. The light waves slow and bend when they hit water. Each color making up the white light has a slightly different wavelength. So, each bends at a slightly different angle. The white light separates as a result, and we see a rainbow overhead!

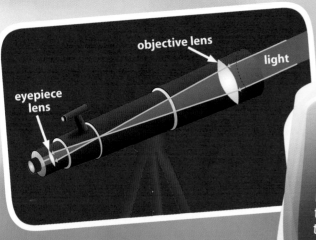

objective lens

light

eyepiece lens

It's All Clear

Like water, glass and plastic also refract light. Refractor telescopes work by focusing these light waves in a particular spot.

Light enters one end of the telescope. The objective lens bends the light to a focus, or point.

The eyepiece magnifies, or enlarges the image.

visible light

Visible light is refracted as it passes through a prism.

violet
indigo
blue
green
yellow
orange
red

What Do You See?

Not all surfaces reflect or absorb light in the same way. We already know that light-color objects reflect more light. They draw our eye and our attention because of this.

Mirage

Many thirsty travelers have been fooled by the effects of refraction on a hot day. A mirage occurs because warm air refracts light rays near the ground. The rays bend upward. The result is the illusion of water in the distance.

Color and Shine

We are much more likely to notice a bright orange cone in the road than a dark gray one. And yellow flowers stand out more than purple ones. But some objects shine despite their color. A brand new black car doesn't look dull. That's because it has a smooth surface. How smooth or rough an object is affects its ability to reflect light. Light bounces off all surfaces. But smooth, even surfaces reflect light in a straight path. That produces a stronger reflection. The reflected light also produces a shiny look.

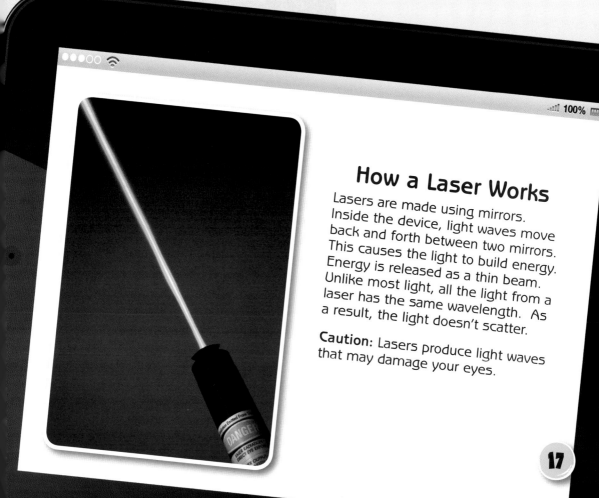

●●●○○ 🛜   .ııll 100% 🔋

How a Laser Works

Lasers are made using mirrors. Inside the device, light waves move back and forth between two mirrors. This causes the light to build energy. Energy is released as a thin beam. Unlike most light, all the light from a laser has the same wavelength. As a result, the light doesn't scatter.

Caution: Lasers produce light waves that may damage your eyes.

Distortion and Scattering

Mirrors reflect light better than any other surface. They reflect light so well that we can see any object that's directly in front of a mirror reflected right back! The polished surface of a new car reflects so much light that it acts almost like a mirror. But if you look at yourself in the surface of the car, your image isn't going to look like the one you see in the bathroom mirror. Objects with curves don't reflect light in a perfectly straight path. As smooth and even as a car's surface is, it's not as flat as your mirror at home. The curves of the car break up the direct path of light. As a result, the reflected light is scattered. Your reflection looks distorted.

Mirror, Mirror on the Wall

There are three types of mirrors. Plane mirrors are simple, flat mirrors like the one in your bathroom. Concave mirrors curve inward. Convex mirrors curve outward.

convex mirror

concave mirror

CRAYONS

Distortion happens with light-colored objects, too. Toasters have shiny, light-colored surfaces, just like mirrors. But the reflections you see in them don't look exactly like you. The curves reflect an odd version of you. **Scattering** creates this effect.

Funhouse mirrors work in the same manner. The mirrors are deliberately curved and warped to produce strange-looking reflections. These mirrors aren't like the flat ones we hang at home to check our appearance.

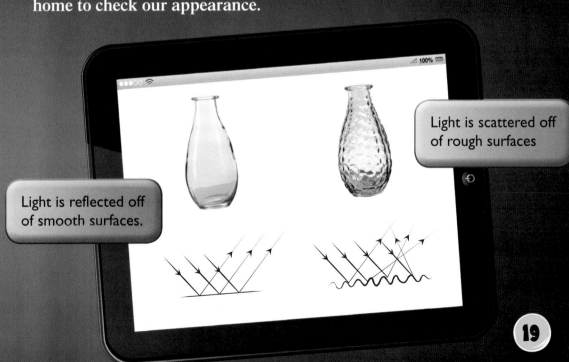

Light is scattered off of rough surfaces

Light is reflected off of smooth surfaces.

Scattering even occurs with objects we would expect to be transparent. When we use glass for windows, light transmits through them. But when glass has texture, it obstructs the light from taking a straight path. Even a small curve in glass will cause light to scatter. As a result, the glass is no longer transparent. These surfaces are translucent. Textured glass is often used for shower doors and bathroom windows because it provides both light and privacy!

Textured glass is a bit bumpy. But some surfaces are so rough that they scatter light in all directions. Consider, for example, the rough bark of a tree. Every slight bump or crack makes the light bounce in another direction. The light we see is so scattered, we can't see the shine of a reflection. That's why a tree's surface looks dull instead of shiny.

In the same manner, a rough, uncut diamond has very little shine. But master jewelers polish and cut the stones to achieve a brilliant shine. They base their designs on their scientific knowledge of reflected light.

glass frog

Onions become translucent when cooked because the chemicals and water in the onions that make them opaque evaporate during cooking.

Translucent and Transparent Animals!

There are animals that are translucent and transparent! Glass frogs are green like other frogs, but they are translucent. You can see their organs through their skin. The glasswing butterfly has transparent wings with brown borders.

glasswing butterfly

Particles of Light

Waves explain most of light's traits. But light can also act as a particle. To see this, we turn to the atom. The atom is a small bit of matter in the world around us. Every object, from our toes to our toys, is made of atoms.

Atoms contain even smaller particles. Neutrons and protons huddle at the center of the atom. Around the neutrons and protons are spaces called *orbitals*. Electrons are located in these spaces. They move inside the orbitals but not in a set path. This means that you never know where an electron will go next. When an atom is energized, its electrons move to higher orbitals. In time, electrons drop back to their normal orbital. To do so, they let go of any extra energy. That energy is given off as **photons**. Photons are the base unit of light. So, a photon is a tiny particle of light.

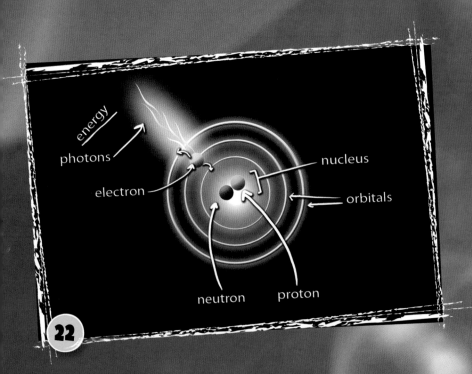

Albert Einstein originally discovered photons, but he called them *energy quanta*. Gilbert N. Lewis was the first scientist to call them *photons*.

electron

Electromagnetic Radiation

The behavior of electrons—giving and receiving photons—is why light is called *electromagnetic radiation*.

So, light isn't matter. It is energy given off by the behavior of electrons. Even so, photons behave like particles when they interact with matter.

Matter can absorb the energy of a photon. When it does, we feel this transfer of energy as heat. Photons are what make the sand on the beach warm. The sand absorbs the photons from sunlight, warming our toes.

Photons also interact with our eyes. When a photon of light meets the eye, it becomes electrical energy. This energy is transferred to our brains to form an image. Photons help us see.

Photons can travel at the speed of light. That's a whopping 299,338 kilometers (186,000 miles) per second! The fastest jet in the world would take 4.5 hours to go all the way around the planet once. But at the speed of light, you could make that same trip 7.5 times. And it would take you only one second.

Light Fight

Light sabers are less science fiction than we once assumed. We always thought photons couldn't interact. But recent research shows that photons can bind together to form molecules. When they interact, they can push against each other and deflect.

Albert
Einstein

Duality

Light can act like a wave and like a particle. This is stated in the wave-particle duality theory. Albert Einstein worked with other scientists, paving the way for this theory.

Power of Light

We take light for granted because it's always present. But imagine what our lives would be like without it! Light gives us sight. It allows us to see color. It provides us warmth. It keeps us healthy. It even helps us communicate.

We know plenty about light. We're aware of the way it's absorbed and reflected to create color. We understand how refraction and scattering cause distorted images. And we know there's a lot more to light than just what the eye can see.

We also know a little about photons and how they affect our vision and the temperature of objects. But light is no ordinary energy. There's so much more left to learn about how it works and what it can do. Scientists still hope to uncover the secret as to how it can act as both a wave and a particle. And they are always seeking new ways to use its power.

"For the rest of my life I will reflect on what light is."
—Albert Einstein

Think Like a Scientist

How does refraction change the appearance of things? Experiment and find out!

What to Get

❯ clear glass jar with lid

❯ magazine

❯ magnifying glass

❯ water

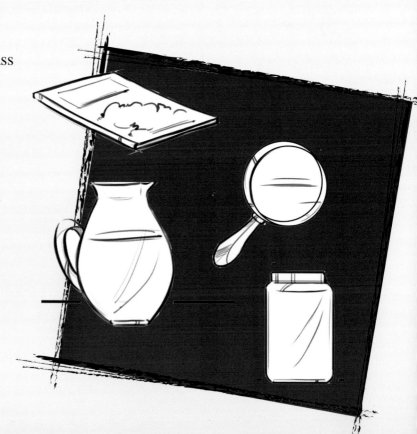

What to Do

1 Fill the jar with water and screw on the lid.

2 Turn the jar on its side and place it on top of the magazine.

3 Begin rolling the jar slowly down the page.

4 How does the jar change the appearance of the text? Would a different size or thickness of jar change the way you see the text?

5 Look at the reading material through the magnifying glass. Does the text look different? What differences in the two materials could change the results you see?

Glossary

gamma ray—a ray that is like an X-ray but of a higher energy and that is given off by a radioactive substance

infrared—electromagnetic radiation with wavelengths longer than visible light but shorter than radio waves

matter—anything that has mass and takes up space

opaque—not letting light through

photons—tiny particles of light or electromagnetic radiation

scattering—the random change in direction of the particles of a beam or wave of light

translucent—not completely clear but clear enough to allow light to pass through

transparent—able to be seen through

ultraviolet—used to describe rays of light that cannot be seen and that are slightly shorter than the rays of visible light

visible spectrum—all the light waves in the range humans can see

white light—light that contains all the colors of the visible spectrum

X-rays—electromagnetic radiation with an extremely short wavelength

Index

Your Turn!

Ever-Changing Color

The strength of the light around you can influence the colors you see. Look at familiar objects at different times during the day. Look at them inside and outside. What changes do you notice? Share your observations with friends and family!